lūminaə

allison marie conway

glory begin publishing

Printed in the United States of America

First Printing, 2018

ISBN (print): 978-0-9977234-2-7
ISBN (e-book): 978-0-9977234-3-4

Cover design by Bri Bruce Productions
Cover photo by Annie Spratt via Unsplash

Glory Begin Publishing
www.allisonmarieconway.com

for john and frank jr.
you are the loves and joys of my life

lumen naturae : the light of the darkness itself

lūminaə

There is a light
which the darkness recognizes
as its own.

It is who we are.

We curse our scars
when all they ever
did
was try
to heal us.

Where you were hurt
where it was not
your fault,
where the butterflies
worked on you
with their kisses
and stitches
and whispered
against your raw
and frightened
openness:

This, my dear child,
this is how
you grow wings.

Here is the flood. Here is everything in me I cannot name. I cannot hold onto any longer. I cannot identify and you will not recognize as me. Here are the ways my mind is deficient. Here are the things I worry about and all the things I wish were different about me but they never will be. Here is the pain, the color of amber glowing fireflies underneath pines; here is my fear of death, it is written in Braille although I can see. Here is my fear of speaking and not speaking, the color of the faces of those who are holding back the same things I am, and this is the way it feels to judge: the color of chains. This is how it feels to be judged.

Here is my mouth covered with black tape, here is my mouth wet with hunger, anger, love, greed, hope. Here is the way I pray, it is the color of midnight, it is the sounding of a word of a God they do not want me to know about because I am made of it; the color of love matches exactly the color of rejection. Reflection and deflection mix, we are without lenses, we use the wrong color eyes. This is the body, my prayer comes alive when we touch in dreams. Here is worship, it tastes like the rain coming down and filling small and large puddles, lakes inside of stones in my mouth, in my shoes, here is all the poetry I have read. It is so much better than what I have done that it liberates and punishes me in equal measure.

Here is the struggle I struggle with, wanting like mad to touch the sky. Wishing like a child when I'm no longer allowed. Crawling like a wounded animal. Chanting like a witch or a monk or a hollow bird. Prisoners. Keys. Book shelving and brittle lace sleeves.

Here are the things about me I do not yet understand. Here are the ways I hide. Here are the ways I want to love you enough that you will never have to die but I need to learn to love you enough that you can. Here are all the things I have learned. Here are all the things I have not learned and I should have. By now. Here is the yellowing of my anguish. Here are the tear stains, I'll trade you anything, but it is too late. Here is the silence of the passing of time. Let's take a drink.

Here are the ways I am not enough. Here are the ways I'll let you forget everything for a while. Here are the things I'd like you never to know. I think somehow it is better you do know, I hope that's okay. Am I a burden? Am I a siren? Am I your muse and will you always think I deserve to be? I hate that this matters to me but I also think it's sweet. Tragedy and comedy, any given day of the week.

This shouldn't be so long. I shouldn't have kept you but sometimes your kindness is so endless I forget who is keeping who around. I love you for that. I hope our changing doesn't change us but how can anything about the truth be helped. We can tie the hands but not ever stop giving. This should not be so . . . *I should not ask this of you.* To look at me. To be seen. To be still. But here is the truth I keep in a small locket underneath my tongue, and I'm sorry before you even come close to it because I don't know who I am, I don't know the color of this thing.

Please understand: I'm showing you things I've not yet seen. It is not fair. If I were to kneel in front of you, bow my head down at your feet, would you know exactly who you are. Would you recognize this as strength and would you be strong enough to lead a leader, to comfort a comforter, to protect the protector, to mother and father the mother and father.

Would we understand each other if there were no sound. What is God but the pain between us understood. Where is this coming from, I don't know. I have only just now noticed my insides, life is becoming an x-ray, a screen, a transfer, though it seems I'm falling into my own hands, these words could be everything, they could be nothing, they could be mindgames, they could be spiritual text to last for all time as soon as they disappear. I would love to fall apart next to you, finally, completely, and have you bear witness, and have you collect me piece by piece by piece.

Are you still glad you came? Are you still because you can see me and it's beautiful or because you are steadying yourself to run. I've lost my instinct, I've lost my ability to collect and interpret the signs, intuition (it turns out) is just free fall. I've given up all the ground I thought I'd won but now I see it was never really there to begin with. How is it that we make terrain out of pride, arrogance, cruelty, and then stake a claim.

Smoke made of walls.

How is it that people can live their whole lives and never know their own names. What is your favorite color and by that I mean what have you seen that has brought you to full orgasm. What do you crave, what turns your mouth to fire, your stomach to claws, what about the way I move makes you want to cry.

This is the flood. I carry it in constant. I am swallowing it over and over and over hoping to spare the world from drowning in a disastrous sea of whatever this is I'm made of, the flood of the human things I would rather you couldn't see.

What will kill us all is held inside, held back, forced down, it churns with the force of a thousand tidal waves, crashing, crashing, crashing upon the inner shores, only to recycle itself and return again.

We walk around afraid of the flood. Pointing out there, out there, out there I see it coming in the red clouds, in the blackgray sky, in the thunder as it rolls up the ground like carpet, in the faces of the ones I cannot understand. *In the other.* But the other is the flood in me. All the human things you cannot see, one day this will end in paradise. One day you will see them all in me.

— here is the flood.

The bravest of all
are the ones
who feel everything.

I see you there
carrying broken hearts
like cuts in your
palms
radiant love
like the tortured
sun.

All sorrow is an invitation.

To be invited into yourself
so deeply
is the fire and trauma
of reconstruction.
Your house will have to break
it will have to burn
before it may
rise.

You curl your fingers around the pieces of you which are filth. And you say to them: I am not leaving you, I will not ever leave you. No matter what, you will know love. And this love will be bigger than we are alone because this love is freedom. Freedom to be joy or sorrow, freedom to scream in the shadows, freedom to be wretched and a disaster.

And suddenly the light breaks through
as if she cannot help herself.

As if finally, at last, the truth became the truth.

And that was enough.

As the pale ticking of a clock slides eternity farther and farther away from my hands—I cannot shake this feeling buried heavy inside my limbs. There is a place where frailty is the beginning of strength beyond anything you have ever seen, where spring green seeds line the inner corners of eyes yet to be born, and it is there you may dream of everything they told you not to dream.

It is within the fabric of this oceanic thing you may breathe air, smoke, water, freedom.

And the voices which call you away cut against the grain. Where light flashes across your nighttime feet and you remember how to move, clumsily at first, hideous at best. From your dying mouth the world away turns, spins out across the purpling abyss. The inner world is the world according to yourself, the smell of rot, the smell of blood, the smell of a lilac tree blooming eroticism at the fullness of season. The scent of firesides lined with snow, winter climbing the legs of empty trees. It is the most exhausting softness you have ever heard.

There is a spirit who moves among even the least spiritual creatures. There are ties that bind us which we refuse to see. And for all the ways we burn each other to the ground it knows that sometimes ashes are the only way we remember how to believe. Will it come on paper boats, will it sound like drums, will the poets find the words in time.

I watch them write about what they tell themselves is love. I see how they stutter against the words they do not know they do not mean. There is a sadness which has hardened into stone, too many hollow people lusting after one another's bones.

— wolves in winter.

I do not think we ever find
what we are looking for.
I do not think
that is the point.
I think it is the search we desire
most.
That part of us which is eternal
is the looking which lives inside
forever.

This god of yours
what if she
is just the fabric of
unending
curiosity.

I have become
all of the silences
you taught me to keep.

— how we build the walls between us.

The silent mouth
of memory;
a flower opens itself
to an empty room.

I think of you
in the light as shade fades
against these gray walls
in the moments that catch themselves like hooks
on the edges of the words
I never spoke
out loud,
in the moments of smoke
amber
and sadness.

We are born
from poetry.
It flowers
in us.

Sunlight dims to gray pretending to fall through the window as I pretend my mind is not so full of madness I can taste the blood in my gums. When we speak of art, of beauty, of the written word, of what do we actually speak? Mostly torture. Mostly the cutting away of every untruth the others cannot even detect. I'm no better at life but I do show up and the showing up is usually what tears the skin off the bone.

They say you have to keep going even in the face of adversity and then they try to convince you that the adversity comes from outside. Look on the walls, they say to you; look into their flush faces, listen to their unbridled hatred. We cannot admit the demons are really on the inside, that the monsters may multiply but they all wear my face.

Gazing into the dresser mirror, I think of the way you left me stronger than you found me and then I question even that. To know you was to love you by untying the fears which kept me pinned to the ground. I came up to the surface for air only to discover you and you were a drowning I wanted more than life itself. Why do we do these things, why do we cringe and sweat over the way certain people kiss with death all stained upon the mouth.

Why do we try, why do we write, why do we peel the mothworn curtains back just to reveal another day. To get to something. And even though we know it's there we fight ourselves to get to it anyway. We the small slits of intimacy, we the sharp unnatural bends in the wing.

When no words worth repeating show up I imagine packing away my notebook and heading back into the world gutted by depletion, rejected even by myself and I know that is the heaviest burden of all. To feel that there is not one single place in all the world—outside or in—where you belong.

Maybe the bad days are just the way too many good ones weigh us down in the quiet moments we never speak about. Maybe they blend the unforgiving sky with the cold rain and even our insides are made of decay. Maybe I just have to wait, and I can do that. I hate it. But here I am, waist deep.

— wading in.

I have made
an entire body of work
out of silence.

— patience.

One of the hardest things for a woman to do
is to let go.
We are so eager to nurture
that sometimes we confuse nature's message
and we continue to try to inject life
into that which must die.
This is a hurt wild and ferocious
for the pains at birth
are the pains of life and death
at once.

One of the hardest things for a woman to do is walk away. From anything. Even the parts of herself which must die in order for her soul to renew itself. She has a terrible time allowing those parts of herself which once inspired her—but now are killing her—to pass away.

We are raised, we are so often told, encouraged, expected, to nurture, nurture, nurture. We the womb within the womb, we the milk of the breast, we the blood and skin of the blood and skin.

But so rarely are we allowed the space and time, so rarely are we empowered by those around us, to understand that to nurture in truth is to know when and how to foster life and when and how to embrace death. That the cycles, beautiful and grotesque, must turn within us. Must rise and fall around us in order for we as women to become all we are meant to become as human beings, as bearers of light, as mysteries of the dark, as wild creatures of nature.

That to allow something to die in its own time with integrity and grace is to give it permission to move fully through life.

Every chapter that begins must come to a close.

Laughter and tears bathe the dirt at the foot of every rose.

— strength of a woman.

There are wars
inside me
I try to keep.

— pain.

You are allowed to write, love.
Just to write.

Not for money or fame or popularity or perfection or acceptance or glory or to prove something or to win something or to fix something or to be better than anybody or less than anybody or to make them happy or proud or right or wrong or repulsed or forgiven or belittled or to make them fall in love with you.

Thinking you have to write what they want you to write is to give your lungs away and think you can still keep breathing. It is to hand over everything that is sacred to your soul and think you will still have something left to give. Social media is mostly a game, a distraction, and a time and creativity suck.

It is not what matters to your art. The writing is what matters.

I have seen terrible writing praised and I have seen beautiful writing ignored. So much of what goes on is an illusion.

They have opinions. They have praise and they have insults. That is what they have and it has not one single thing to do with your writing. Why you do it, how you do it, is up to you.

You write because the writing is yours.

The writing is always yours.

This sadness
seems to
need me.

— tender.

Have you any idea
the strength it takes
to be this
tender.

(For the ones who bear
the anguish of the world
like a bruising inside
their very souls
and open their arms
to it anyway.)

What they do not want you
to ever know
to ever be comfortable inside
is that you are
enough.

Because once you know that
really know it in the marrow of your bones
you can no longer be
manipulated
sold to
lied to
destroyed
abused
cursed
depleted
controlled
disheartened
dismantled
discouraged
stopped
patronized
held back
held off
held hostage.
And when all of this
is off the table
the world will have no idea
what to do with you
where to put you
how to keep your wild beautiful
voice down.

I had been given too many hands, brought up with ravens nesting in my throat. Love is screaming down the hall, love is darkness tearing cracks in a house which cannot fall. I learned the secret as it was threaded, woman into woman into woman into me. My wrists rush full of your veins (you at the ankles of my budding devotion, you the ascending lotus flower, you the sinew of the mouth of lineage).

My name is a language, my name is a generation, my name is earth, my name is seven letters penned in the dirt.

My name is the name of the truth.

I made it split my tongue, this opalescent rain which fills my lungs. Wet this room at the center of my neglect, concave, dim; the white eyes of this dying celestial.

Fracture this calculated light where I hunger and crawl and thirst for the rivers, watch as my numbness scales every mountain if only to peel back the sky; death is but a kiss along the seabed of a withering moon. Teacher, read for me. If my words disturb you, feed your breath to the cells of my body until I speak again of gentleness, speak the name, all of the names within my name, embryos falling through my hands.

And we will turn our cold minds to emptiness; we will coax a taste for morning, begin to raise our faces from the dust.

— rise.

Perhaps wounds
are just love
bloomed too soon.

And what will you do to dig up these bones when I'm still here, how will you feed me to the wolves who need my throat, teach me, grow me with their yellow marks and claws. Suddenly it is all black water in this garden, the water rises and churns, setting the tides on fire and I am swimming deeper and deeper still until I find those things I lost so long ago, milkteeth, crickets, the shadows I crawled into behind my childhood eyes, before the waste of the world became so tired and overgrown, before it was the cold which stung like bees, before it was the heart I bled underneath my sleeves.

The people don't come back, they walk onward, they walk past, I weep for I would do the same, and have. The spaces in between my lungs (naked lungs severed and hanging from trees) there are wings fluttering there, little bodyless commotions, threadbare ivory wings who meant to reach for the burned out sun but fell blind, and I swallowed them whole.

No one to tell in hushed dry tones, no one to tease open my waterfall lips, no one to paint their ears on again, only doors into an ancient unhinged soul who is always leaving and does not bother to lock up anything.

Unchained, unrattled, untethered, untouched. This flesh was made for letting
go
of.

There is a dark moon which rises alone in every heart, it cannot move, only reflect, it cannot breathe. And as these nights cave the days in upon me, I do not reach, I do not reach. Bury me, all these beautiful little moth wing lights sifting down as I do not speak. All of these gentle lights burying me.

— gentle lights, bury me.

The body sometimes
stays
in place
of the heart.

— (dis)appearance.

allison marie conway

This hunger within
even as it is
eating me
alive
when did these bones
of mine
become so much
fade.

Had this come at a better time I would have placed my hands into your hands and we would have forgotten who was holding on to who. Instead I lower my eyes as your eyes close and bow to the end of whatever we had between us constructed. Little melting paper tissue promises, we traded words wrist over wrist, your mouth warm upon my alabaster skin.

I am the draining of the cup, I am the small child who writes only of leaving, only of the lightning in dark clouds. How even the slenderest tears streak the breast with fire before running aground.

I am picking at my fingernails and you are staring out the window of a neon train as my legs begin to burn. I used to dream I was covered in red ink and the more closely I inspected the skin the higher the vines of crimson would curl up and up across my stomach, my chest, my neck, and then I would awaken, awash in thrumming laps of sweat.

And here we are together parting ways, two hearts divided in ten thousand ways.

I watch as the gray buildings of the city sink slowly into the raging sun. I think of all the people reaching for something they do not understand and missing it like hell anyway.

Why do they think everything destructive is so pretty
and that everything pretty
is not them.

— merry go round.

I lose myself
too easily
even in
the
light.

It is not enough, is it, even if I could turn these wallshadows into fruit, even if my body were the dark burst of blackberries between your tongue and your enemy's teeth, stain the bed sheets with your lips.

Even if the way I touch you riddles the sunlight across the window; little flashes burn through the fog around your cheeks,

the way we feed each other on this thin selection of time,

is this your breath I pull across my mouth, is this the rib I borrowed from the birds you hold in your hands (one is sorrow, one is freedom). It is always you, you inside me as I

write what hangs from the trees in dreams. Who am I to hope for anything when the world is on fire. Who will they send for us if we do not emerge again. Love is on the drinking cup, love is on the fountain top, love is the bottom of roses gummed to shoes.

Take me with you into the familiar warmth, take me back to the way it was before, when I told the truth and you would believe me. You

wanted to believe

me.

Now it's only the green mornings they tell me I should smile upon; they keep telling me not to blink, throwing hurricanes in my eyes, and raise my useful hands

up to the sky (but it is hard because she's falling

as I am falling, and we

can't seem to touch)

and I'm so tired, there's never much good in telling a thing when you are very tired.

Everybody wants to be so heavy, so full of metal skyline and mysterious things. What is that worth to you? Where is it getting you to summon up the truth?

The hair on your head still itches.

The gums you hold together in your jaw still bleed.

— love is on the drinking cup.

And I think to myself
after all this
after all the skies threw themselves
down your throat
and you were drowning
in your own
skin
and the hurricanes made blindness
of your eyes
your hands
your voice,
here you are.
Here you are
the guardian of worlds
the daughter of
a miracle.

I have tried
to eat my own beauty
swallow the blood
on my hands
to hide
the starving.

— hidden.

It's all around you, the way the vacant words falling from the mouths of those who do not understand separate and resuscitate themselves, surviving only barely by the eating of your breath.

You like the rainy days because they break you and cradle you just enough. I can tell you wear anguish and destruction like a shield, that you believe safety is a gag and a blanket, something you win by paying for it with every aching fiber of who you want to be.

When you smile I want to pull the flowers from your bleeding chest and plant them in the darkest corners of my mind. Never to forget you, you and all of your wilderness, all of your seasons of life and skeletons and death. A wall of tears is suspended in the air, at any moment about to crash along the surface of your limbs. You can tell me all the dirty things, I have no interest in robbing them of you.

The moment I met you I knew we had known each other for a very long time, it felt like my eyes resting behind your eyes would have made perfect sense. The way you saw the majestic and the terrible things I could see and did not turn away. I am always so taken by the souls of those who find silence to be rich, the ones who slide their bodies into a quiet room and listen for the things most people throw away by moving too fast, protruding too intrusively, talking too much. Saying nothing about nothing when I hunger for so much.

They shuffle and speak in low tones as you drift past their illusions and up into the blue electric sky. It's not that you don't care it's just that there has to be more than this, something with a deeper soul must exist if only people would let the darkness into the light and the light into the places where they think there is nothing more to see.

And as they keep trying to sell us eternity, we fade farther and farther into retreat. This moment, the one catching you and I by the gap between heartbeats, this is the only one we need.

— had I never met you.

To feel so deeply
and not ever want
to give that up.

— the gift.

and the years are falling
down the street
as all the lonely hearts
fold their melancholy songs

against the milk bare
sky.
the echo of evening
at the heels of their feet.
little lights are coming on
all over the globe
and my breath is the smoke
of the way you spoke
of moving on.

my hands still resemble
the shape of you.

And then
don't explain
any of it.

I had been imagining a house
detached
coming off the hinges
of itself.
Inside where the people
are very beautiful
and they are
not speaking.
Their tongues have all been broken
by the jaws of much
too much
to say.
And there in quiet makeshift rooms,
the halls of footsteps grinding on stairs,
indecision,
medication,
fear of spiders and
wire hooks,
in the cold chambers of their slender shadow hearts,
black birds are singing human words
we would recognize as symbols.
Silent are these people
in their lovely cut out houses,
trapped together
falling apart.

— still life.

We are all human which is to say we are all a wild ridiculous miracle. We are all an impossible beauty and madness.

We are here because we have something we must give. It is a creative thing, an artful expression, a uniqueness. A strange paradox wherein what makes us different connects us to each other.

Some kind of seed, some kind of magic.

And it is that gift, that treasure, that spark, which we seek with abandon and ache in the deepest recesses of our being, the essence of who we are.

I keep coming back to this in my own life and experience, that the most radical and restless desire of every human being, what we all truly seek, is to give. This passion of the soul is the fabric of our nature and has not one single thing to do with greed, though we are made to feel guilty when we should not. It is not greedy this soul-seeking hunger because our deepest need, deeper than any need to acquire or impress or control, the deepest need of all is to have something to offer, to express, to share.

We are creatures with an innate, intuitive, primitive, pressing need to give ourselves away. Made of something unseen which is capable of filling and draining itself, of life and death and rebirth. Perhaps there is nothing more heart wrenchingly beautiful.

They ask me why
I write so much
about being
gentle
and I say,
Because we are
at war,
are we not?

At war with our bodies
our minds, our hearts
our neighbors, our friends
our fears, our dreams
our images, our shadows
our demons, our jobs
our lives
our death
our anxieties
our health
our ambitions
our abuse
our neglect
our beauty
our flaws
our family
our country
our history
our beliefs.

There is nothing we
do not rail against
at any given moment.

And yet
we are here.
Here we are trying to
do our best
to laugh at fate
and hold each other close
and lift the broken faces
up to the sun.

And it is important to prove

allison marie conway

that we can fight
peacefully,
too.

— warrior.

You may take my words
twist them
curse them
tear them down
off the walls
but the truth
will still
be mine.

— keep.

All the ways
I did not know
how to love you
catch fire in my throat

wounds poured into salt
along my matchstick tongue.
What was that beautiful pain
sewn to the hips of your acrid words

I open for the taste
of tears tucked under the edges
of my sleeves,
this heart for you

bleeds of longing
wet with need.

Bluegolden bruise,
there is nothing more sincere.

How the color drinks its own skin
just to twist in the crush
of its thirst.
What is this poison

you treat me to.

In this darkness, I will write the sounds of you from the back
of the voices in my body. I will close my mind around you as
the twilight haunts the neighborhood, the streets underneath the
sidewalk all lead to a single window, glowing full of the sky above
your heart. My eyes close around your silence, sleeping in this
dream of life, eternity in a cold black place without walls, a room
without beginning on a bridge overlooking the end.

Baby, where are we, where is it we are climbing to.

But you do not speak. Hair all shades of the wind.

Every morning
flickers of night
resist the dawn
and I
have to learn again
to be gentle
with myself.

— surrender.

It is phenomenal
the way life opens up
when you begin to live
like you are allowed
to be here.

You are allowed to be here, my love. Your joy and your pain are allowed to be here. You do not have to cut away pieces of yourself so that someone else fits and you disappear. You are allowed to take up space and have emotions and feelings and struggles and pretty parts and ugly parts and parts you do not understand yet and parts you want to discover and parts you want to heal but they are still a mess but you are getting there and you are allowed to move and breathe and stretch and try and learn and fall and have thoughts and opinions and ideas and trials and epiphanies and mistakes and victories and do your life all the way as far and as tall and as deep and as wide as you want. All of this. All of this is yours. And you can occupy all of it in full with grace and awkwardness all at the same time.

The way your
silence
lives in me.
The way it tears
at the veins
when it speaks.

Tracing the curve of my left shoulder with your tongue you whisper your obsession with my feathered tattoo and the way my hair smells of cream linen and musky autumn warmth. I am trying desperately to tear my mind into shreds to keep her quiet and let me spread into what is sure to come next if I could just let go.

It is a hard thing to manage when the world is falling to hell more quickly now than ever before. Every word is a promise and promises break. It is so much more brutal to have to tell the truth when the truth is that half the time humanity makes no sense to me, that despite all the trimmings we hang upon the walls of the houses we build in our hands, nothing seems to be able to ease this restless burden most of us have become.

You lay me down and look at me like maybe you think I am the answer. The impossible beauty of your heart watches patiently as my body becomes the earth and my veins become rivers of thin pewter floods rushing out in all directions. I am a sea creature, I am a weather vane, I am the sobs of your childhood nightmares finally slinking down through the floor.

You are a kind of safety I am afraid to know. So many people live like lives should all be the same, they skim the surface and eat it and eat it and eat it instead of admitting they have been starving since birth because they are afraid to die. Push each other down, push it all away, press the dry burning leaves against the fractured window panes.

As you bury yourself into me my eyes catch upon a sliver of the sky, screaming blue. As though even the heavens do not believe our anguish.

— the world in your hands.

What scares me most
is I might
be
worth
everything.

— and, oh my love,
what might you do then.

As the flash of another day burns the tall glass buildings down to graystone, we move closer to each other like an uncomfortable evening fog. You are whiskey and I am torn blue jeans. We are both bare feet and distraction.

We are together even when we are apart, an impossibility it would seem, and so very far apart when we are together.

What is it?

I can feel it. The weight of too many worlds hanging like lead from your tired limbs. You can be sad here. I will not sweep the graypain in our midst away. *Show me.*

Open your wounds in front of me and I will not crumble, I will not break. I will not disappear.

Even from across the room I can see your light. I promise it is not gone.

Have I ever told you that I think you are stronger than the others for coming undone? Forget what they have told you, to unravel is not easy. It might be madness but it is real, the way we close ourselves tight around secrets we no longer have to keep. Love is barbed wire, love is midnight falling along the trees.

Tell me the mess about yourself that you do not understand. About the dreams which seem to fall away from you as you reach for them across the strange pulsewaves in your mind. I know it is hard sometimes. I know it hurts to be alone and yet all you want in all the world is to be unafraid of being alone.

Tell me how the aching in your heart feels like rainfall sliding down the gutters of your clouded eyes. I want to know how the cold feels the way only you can feel it, how the snow upon your bare skin sometimes rests warm like springtime even though no one seems to understand.

I believe you. Everyone has their troubled bones but no one else *has yours*.

So tell me about the sorrow that carves away at you; tell me what seems to ruin your touch and dissolve your breathing. Tell me the lies and the truth and how you are ashamed of both, and we will sort through whatever it is that cries at the center of your soul, at the tips of your fingers, at the back of your throat.

Tell me what it is to be so gruesomely, ironically human.

Speak for me the terrible quiet burden of this mad beautiful life.

— superhuman gifts.

*Everyone has
their troubled bones
but no one else
has yours.*

Perhaps the most powerful
thing
you can do
is own your desire
instead
of shaming it.

We get caught sometimes
between who we were
and who we think
we should become.
The answer, the magic,
is in letting go
of both.

Learn about who you are now. Taste all of where you have been as it brushes up against your skin but no longer binds you. So many have come before you, angel. So many lives and bodies to bring you forward, so many miracles that you may sit here and hold a poem in your hands.

There is so much, so much, so very much that you are. You are rich, you are flowering and whispering, and flowing. You are so many wild and ecstatic things no one else can see.

Dive deep into your depths just exactly as you are, as you live and breathe and occupy that beautiful body, that magnificent mind. Remember yourself to yourself. And for now, be content that you have always been and will forever be soul.

Can you not feel this
ache,
beloved,
this half-living on top
of the skin,
this coming so close
and not being invited
in.

— self reflection.

Then there were all the ways
we never found what we were looking for.
We did not know its color or
how to recognize its sound.

The way the lights descended from the heavens
and filled us so bright until the dark
felt like home again.
The home to light is darkness,

they belong inside of one
another and become
a single swaying being
no one knows how to speak about.

And so the silence, on one specific invisible day
and not one day before,
begins gathering twigs and little bones of
things deceased,

assembling her nest inside the
blinding noise.

And this is how we burn our lives away
waiting for daybreak
hiding behind the sky.

Expansion.

Detachment.

Release.

— behind the sky.

There is no amount of loathing
which can give birth
to the healing it needs.
You cannot beat love
out of you.

— self compassion.

My strength has not
one single thing
to do
with violence.
Can you
understand that.

— strength.

But it's my softness
that will kill you.

Truly powerful people
are so gentle
when they come close to you
that the anguish inside you dies
and you breathe
and you fall open
and in their presence
in the sheer beauty of their disarmament
you give yourself over to the love
you did not think
you deserved.

Maybe we just want them to know
we were here.
Maybe we don't really want
to be pretty
it's just that we
are afraid if we are not
then it's like we
never existed
at all.

— how we (do not) see women.

Someone once told me I write like a storm, like something is chasing me, like I have to get the words out before time is up. I don't know if that's true, I don't know if that is a lovely or a ridiculous thing. I don't really think it matters anyway because if you are going to write you must write from the inside, not from the outside looking in. It will be what it is.

All I know is that I am woven of a deep and pressing need to give, to pour forth. I am consumed with words and a ferocious desire to love madly.
I was always so.

But when I was young I had no where to pour forth the way I was dying to, the way I was designed to; it was too much for most people to bear.

Too much love, I was to learn, could crush a person into silence, into leaving me, into being angry with me, into turning away from me.

And so I've carried on with the keeping of secrets, and my darkest secret is Love. Don't you see that? The darkest secret of all the world is Love.

The love in the shadows, the love in the dark, the love withheld, the love held back, the love denied, the love buried, the love shamed, the love abused.

All the poetry never written is the dark seed of a Love so wild and so strong most dare not breathe up close to it. But close to it is the only place I want to be.

I want my body and soul wet with dark soil.

Because I did not come here to run from the storm.

I came to run with it.

— storm.

Why poetry?

Because that word
has always brought me
the most joy.

— all the reason
you ever need.

You are a universe
all by yourself.

To say
the hard things
softly
without losing
their weight.

— wisdom.

When everything is a mess
and the world around you is wretched
and in your heart you feel hate
and rage and shame and nastiness
you are not supposed to talk about
and you are angry and beaten and broken
all at the hands of your own goddamn self

you will write.

And then you will know what it is
to reach beneath the rage
and find just enough love
to be where you are
and not judge
and not injure
and not run.

— non-violence : why we do this.

When we create
we give way
to ourselves.

This is the terror.
This is the gift.

I know you are afraid of what
you are made of, what lies
sleeping inside the bones.
I know the way it wants to make infinite love
to you
and how you curl up inside your
ribs
recoiling from touch.
The rage, the heat, the dark.
How beautiful
how beautiful
how beautiful
are you.
What comes from you
rejects you.
What pours forth
runs dry in canyons down
your lonely skin.
But this, too, is the freedom, child.
The salt upon your tongue
will keep you thirsty.
The salt upon your tongue
is the fire in the eyes
which keeps you young.

I hope you are not
holding back,
my dear.
Not your love
not your beauty
not your wilderness.
This broken world
cannot afford
your withholding.

— hope.

Slow down.
Let me look
at you.
Let me hold
your presence
taste the burdens
on your skin.

— to pay attention.

And the way you spoke
like a rainflower
b r o k e n o p e n
beauty rushing thick
from your tongue.

Even the light
you fed me
was poison
but I was too hungry
to see.

Starvation
whether of the body
of the mind, or of the spirit
is a cruel and dangerous thing.
It is violence which breeds
more violence.

In our desperation we will reach
for anything we can find
to ease the sharp clench
of the hunger pains.

To fill ourselves
where we have too long been voids.

(We fear violence because we neglect where it begins.)

How much we have
to wash away
hands
eyes
tongues
to get to ourselves.

— cleanse.

Last night
I dreamt of you.
When did you
walk into me
so deep.

Do not add to your pain by blaming
yourself for what they call "low self esteem."
We were raised on poor self esteem.
We were rewarded for it. It was
sewn into our backs
before we had a voice.
Our wrists
were opened
and it was injected into our veins.

It is only when you forgive yourself
you realize you must cleanse yourself
of what you do not own
but what was
hung around your neck
what was
pressed through your throat
what was
bound to your ribs
to keep you
from flight.

— freedom.

Beautiful creature
free yourself.

Write all that is yours
to write.
Be grateful.
Do it again.

— how to be a writer.

By the gentle press of rain
which slopes at the gray window
of morning,
there is hot tea

and all I'm dreaming of
is you.
You, the dusty wings
of the patience of days

to come.
You, the way dark winter trees
stand still against
a white ghost sky.

Freedom of flight, nothing
to hide.
You, the familiar hand I hold
underneath warm feather pillows

late at night.
Maybe love is just a strange
surprise
that lasts forever.

All the painful places
I dared to let you touch
became flowers
gardens blooming
from broken earth
for the gentle
 of your sun.

— healing.

When you are here
it is
all poetry.

How dangerous
this woman
who trusts herself.

— out of line.

You see the words—
the words and I
we are obsessed.

Here are
your hands.
They will mend
or dismantle
you.

— choice.

We have become something
unspeakable.
Something which eats
itself.

— greed.

For what are shadows
but servants
of the light.

What I think many don't understand is that a writer is always turning back toward the writing. That we are either in that space, in that 'other' space which we occupy alone, which we sink into with such reverence and need, or we are trying to get back to it, trying to understand and pull pieces out of the sky which belong to it.

We are an eternal return, an infinite homecoming.

It's like we have a little invisible drawer where we keep the sacred special secret things and we keep bringing bits back: bits of nature, of emotion, of light, color, taste, texture, sound, impulse, desire, hunger, heartbreak, anger, fear, whatever—everything. Imagery, science, the painting on the wall in a dream—everything.

And we are trying very earnestly to make sure we don't miss any of it, not one thing, not one blade of grass or shadow or skinned knee. Not one memory or insight or glimpse of this One divine thing which we don't know, but we know.

We know and we don't know, that's the mystery, that's why we gather so many things—we don't know how or why but we know they go together, somehow. Somehow all things go together, they fit, they hinge.

All things, all creatures, all words are turning back into themselves, there is an order threading through the chaos.

We know it on some level which grips at the veins. That the puzzle has no edges but it does have seams and this is where the magic is, in the creases.

Somewhere in the fitting together of the random bits, we find peace, we find meaning.

We do not know where the work will take us, but we know this is our work.

— where we go home.

Everything will fall away.
Even the beautiful things.
This will be the beginning.

— regeneration.

It's so beautiful to see you out there trying with the cracks in your forehead and the whispering feather lines just beginning to form around the corners of your mouth. The days are a quiet crystal snow falling upon us, we are buried soft, cold, slow. But somehow you keep that light in your smile and your chest.

Don't let them frighten you, heaven is the most ordinary of things. A slate gray sky and nothing to prove any longer. No more reason to rage against the falling out of time.

I wish I could sleep. I haven't slept in ages, I just sift through blackened hallways of the night which calls to me in fire, in butterfly wings made of excitable circles.

Enough about my crumbling. Tell me how you are. Tell me what hurts. Tell me everything. What does it feel like inside that porcelain skin? Isn't this mad rain the soak of the end of time? Wouldn't that be lovely and a relief?

Please forgive me. Something in the rise of your face takes me back to infancy, to helplessness and greed, to a love so innocent that the feeding only makes it hungry.

This woman in me, she is the tilting sand in the hourglass, a ring of wax candles, weeping and singing for the clouds which cover the moon. Her veins are a river of planets, deep angel blue.

This is yours, wear it inside out, hold it close as God and then set it free. This is a season which has come for letting go.

Thank you for being here. I'm so glad you came, this garden is only iron wire and rust without your stories. I think you are beautiful and it is okay to be awkward for your entire life. No one else's eyes bend like yours, but I bet you hear that all the time. I think you are beautiful even with my eyes closed.

Now maybe try to get some sleep.

— how you are.

We tell ourselves we must take care
of the whole world
before we can take care
of ourselves.
As if we have to earn
our own affection
by making it impossible
to reach.

— self care.

You tell me
I only have to give up
a little of who I am
for this to work.
I tell you
my soul does not come
in pieces.

— whole.

You hear life
in my words.
They come from
the mouth
of my blood.

— open.

I am afraid of the way
I swallow beautiful things
and let them die
inside me.

If you think you need them
to approve of you
you have not done
the necessary work
of unburdening your own heart.

Go back inside.

Listen to yourself.

Begin again.

Begin again.

Begin again.

Begin again.

Where I have chewed my own tongue.
Where I have beaten my own truth
back into my bones
and kept quiet my rage.
The place in my psyche
where I murder myself
to please you.
This
is where
I am bruised.

— the pain you cannot see.

Whose game are you playing
when you trade
your deepest desires
for their greatest fears.

— game over.

If you are going to tell me
the truth
tell it to me all the way
to the end.
Tell it so complete
that when we turn around
and look over it
it is impossible to go back
to the way it was
before the telling.

I like the way certain words feel in my body when I write them, the way they form in my hands as a connection to something which could only take place while writing a poem.

Poems, you see, they breathe, they have their own wingspan and depth, they occupy a space, they have an existence in and of themselves. Whenever I am blocked or feeling unprolific I try to remember that we are like two butterflies endlessly encircling each other.

Sometimes you have to wait for the poem; sometimes it has to wait for you.

You will not always be ready at the same time. That is why you have to be in love with the words.

You have to be willing—joyful even—to wait.

I hope you did not think
there were rules.

There is comfort
in letting them decide.
It is false comfort.

The words come as I
forget to eat and try
to catch them.
Sand falls through time.
I hope you dream
bigger than this.
I hope that you do
not give up
or turn to face
the darkness
without tucking your fingers
into the hands
of the light.

Hold them close when they
are madness
let their voices sing in your mind
when they
leave you
for dead.
The people who come too close
are afraid.
The ones who leave
still teach if you can learn
not to let fear
take you under.
This life as she
looks you in the eye

is falling away
from under your feet.

Do not stop.

Do not give up.

Do not keep the words in drawers.

But if you need to
go away for a long time
and let the sea kiss you
all over.

— kiss you all over.

We stay behind ourselves
cowering
when we should
be standing.

You will have to unlearn
what you have been taught
in order to discover
who you are.
To have the courage and compassion
to look inside and see
that you have come to be of
love and of hate.
That you are both sides of light
and of darkness
and to experience for the first time
the depths of the anguish
it takes
to choose love.

— discovery.

In the quiet moments.
This is where I am
richest.

What are the skies like where you are, has the new air been good for you. Blue as the veins of the ocean tide, sweet as the almond sun. The way you look through the way I looked away. Do you bathe yourself with the salt of the tears in my hands, drink your tea warm with honey and is it sunset by the window, or everywhere. I hold your motion in the poetry, feel blindly the depths of the things I cannot touch. You enter me and leave your heart behind. Do you taste my hair against your strawberry mouth and draw the purple shades of night down with your low dark eyes.

I miss the lifetimes I spent alone,
someone's always calling
but no one ever calls me home.

Could it be that we all reach for something like wind to keep us alive when the rest of the world smells only of rot, remains, annihilation. No two souls have ever touched each other inside such gentle bruising. How your teeth never quite leave my flesh days after, the way my voice fills your mind, dampens your tongue, breaks wild against your muscle. How I pray for your healing as I do for you to ache until it bleeds. Nobody says what they really mean.

When you move your body it speaks of the secrets you keep from everyone but me. Lights coming up all over the jagged bones of darkness. The drench of this heady stolen quiet smothering the bedtime trees.

Desire presses in my skin. Beating hot, beating slow.

— slow blood.

I find more people
in deep pain
not because they lack love
but rather they are
so full of love
they are choking on it
because somewhere along the
way
they were taught
it was safer
to punish it
than let it out.

This is why great writers
do not write
and the fires of war
refuse to burn out
and the most beautiful
lovers
in all the world
do not show up
or leave
without saying
goodbye.

Somehow writing from a place of ache
feels also like calling forth
a companion for it.
.

The anguish and the writing
(whatever it is
which
does the writing)
seem to share the same ribs
the same blood.
.

Somehow their resemblance
of each other
becomes kindred.
There is some existential plane
wherein they touch.
.

Where
there is no separation.
So that even the loneliness
has something to
hold onto.

I will not spend my life
(my dignity, energy, creativity)
trying to fit into something
I did not build.
I will bring to life
a design they have never seen
because my eyes were born
hungry for it.

— hunger.

When I write
I raise myself
from the dead.
All the beauty
they cut away from me
begins to bloom again.

— rebirth.

This terrible feeling
a longing which screams
in the veins
cries tears of fire in the blood
why do I
seek it.

— inside.

Why before you
do I open like fruit.
Why
before you
do I blush.

Be gentle.
We all have dreams
and scars.

I loved you
the way a flower
offers her mouth
to the rain.

— I loved you
        this way.

Maybe they will wait for a little while longer to see if the birds return. Mouthing their warm bodies against the hood of the cold. The turning of a doorknob in a crystal champagne room, fall your face into my hands, fall down the rabbit hole, fall up inside the stars. These words you take are the breath of me, my breath a mere illusion.

Please do not. My fragile blood cannot bear the chime of your laughter, that smile of yours will surely peel my skin from the silk of her cloth. It is dark inside the nest I built of shadows, the light and the darkness always forbidden and undressing themselves here, always one without the other, always both speaking at once.

The ticking of a clock: footsteps.
Time is running out
and in
on us.

When it all slows down we are made to face ourselves. It hurts like hellfire behind the eyes when the sun swells so. I used to write like morning dew and now I write like the gray grass beneath the dying, always trembling, always on the heels of the ashes of leaving. Drinking the hips of melancholy static, this is the way I was sewn into a body which never quite fits.

It will be love, I know, I know, it will be love which tears me away from you.
Love laid bare on the wings of a soul adrift, love the rain in the iron garden;
love the silent water bathing night among the reeds.

— this time, away, away.

You told me I
was ugly
so I made myself pretty
then you told me
I was arrogant.

And all the while
it was never
up to you.

In some sordid way
we have each sought
rejection.
For the things we did not have
the courage to leave
to leave
us.

All the vacant people
what occupies their sorrow.

What cruel winters
fall cold upon the white
linen faces

buried in their
minds.

— vacancies.

I love you.
Let me go.

Has this been the hurt inside of you
these cuts on my hands
the crush of broken promises.
Your static mouth a shrieking fog

buzzing in my head, humming—
you like grains of sand
scratching a desert
in my throat.

Remember me a grapefruit moon

hanging in your rearview mirror
love in the back seat
melon. sunset. smoke.
love

took a back seat.

Now the morning rolls down her sheets
silicone heat waves sweat across my tongue.
I listen for you but all that moves nails along the wall
are reflections of an empty afternoon.

(my arms reach
for three corners from this corner)

The windows are swallowing sunlight
the sunlight is dangling through trees
traces of a dim lit landscape
you used to speak of

in dreams.

— remember me.

There you are
like some kind of
disturbance
some kind of
grace.

The way you opened
my body
just to thread these
chains through
me.

— bound.

They could not understand you.
That is what I understood
about you most.

I love the way beauty
does not frighten you.
How you walk unafraid
into daylight;
bend with such unparalleled grace
into the arms
of the crippling
night.

— beautiful.

We write because
no one ever told us
these things
would happen.

The amount of pain
we hammer into our own
bones
and wonder why
the world is
broken.

You cannot skip over
self love, angel.
It's the only love
there is.

Sometimes I catch myself
the words in my mouth
came from yours
and I
wonder exactly
when that happens.

— catch.

Please go slow.
I have trouble believing
the good things
are mine.

It had been a jasmine evening which left its hand upon my chest,
the moon so lonely I could taste her forlorn eyes. Some days prick
like lemondrop needles sweet and bitter against the tongue.

Out there the wolves.
Out there the doves.

Out there a world revolves around itself and the same revolution
envelopes whatever this cruelty is inside of me. I can hear you
talking but I cannot let you in. There was something they gave me
to take away the pain and it took you, too.

I am letting go.

The tethers are coming up
ever so slow
but I still hold you deep in my bones
even if I cannot touch you
this I know
this
I know.

My ribs full of roses blossoming thorns
swollen sadness she is breaking my soil she is
she is mine,
beautiful are the tears which do not come and I know

I'll have to crawl up out of this grave
somehow
swallow life again but this baptismal throat is fire,
these limbs, how we have become this tired.

I do not know.
I do not know.

— jasmine.

We wait
we are so very pretty
in our waiting.

Cross your fingers,
hold your breath,
remove your
eyes.

There is a gnawing in my cheeks which
never stops,
it is keeping sound
with the rippling in my
water glass,
it is
waiting for the other

shoe to drop.

And as the sky turns to blood
and trickles down the insides
of my thighs like
sandpaper before the wallpaint
even dries,
we do believe

what we are told.

Sitting for portraits,
sitting for decades, sitting for
no one.

We are so very pretty
growing old.

— (dis)obedience.

Writing is an act
of connection
in a disconnected world.

Tell me the lies and the truth
and how you are ashamed
of both
and we will sort through
whatever it is
that cries at the center
of your soul.

I am every contradiction
they try to pretend
does not exist.

I am brave and I am
afraid.
I am joyful and I am
uncertain.
I am grateful and I am
insatiable.
I am broken and I am
burning my light
in the dark.

— all at once.

And I know sometimes you will forget
that all creation takes its time
to unfold.

Please do not despair, my love.
This unfurling will be slow.

This is part of what makes it so
beautiful.
Little movements
little breaths
little steps.

But we forget,
we forget,
we forget

to trust the process.

All things of love
bloom
in their own mysterious time.

Go gently upon your
delicate life.

I had tried to speak to you
but the trains all fell from their tracks
and the sky seemed to bleed
its bluebruised heart

between the words in my mind
and the numbness which
grabbed stiff hold of
my tongue.

So if you could just be patient
and not give up on not
letting go
I swear I will be coming home

and it will be so soon
and it will be so crushingly beautiful

like our toes in the
dunegrass and the tiny birds running
along the ocean sunlight
sing.

I know that right now it is quiet
in the night
as you feel the heat
sloping itself through open summer
windows.

Tender sweat has dampened your
alabaster skin
like tears
a whole body cries.

I know the silence hurts more than
any other

sound.
But please remember

I am still here, my angel.

In the stillness of the moonlight
in the handwritten pages
you hold to your
chest.
In between your sweet breathing

and your bothered
fitful dreaming,
you and I
through all the words and beyond them,

and beyond them
even
still,

we are forever bound.

— the bluebruised heart.

If it is not humble
it is not strong.

I had been expected
to laugh
as I was being torn
away from
myself
and to understand
that it was okay
with them
if my smile
was just a blanket
over shattered
bones.

— when I learned (how to split in two).

There is a softness in me so strong
it could disarm the entire universe
in a single breath.

Do you
not see that, my love?

That all of these wars
all of this hatred and cruelty
has grown out of
their terrible fear

of the strength and might
and power
of the way my softness
would shatter all brutality
to dust.

I would dare them all
to take what they had
been given
and make it
poetry.

You have to let
the words come
and show you
who you are.
Bravery and tenderness
must occupy
the same breath.

luminae

After the dance
at the foot of the sun
there is a sadness
twisting inside.

It is a pale scarf
tied to the bedpost.
It is sitting graypain
by the window petalsnow
as we dress.

We do not
speak it.

Silence is the only true poetry.

A poet is the rare
creature
who has found the beauty
in having been
rejected
by this world.

Tell me about the dance. How you have drawn chalk lines on the floors but all they ever did was spin in circles and trample one another's feet. Spread your hands all over me and let me feel the chill of the voices. How has it been to see in the clouds what has become of the poets, the way people panic now behind a cross of stones. Ever since your song has been laid to rest they all pretend they have forgotten how to sing. Perhaps it makes it easier to imagine you are not here.

But I still sing as I tap sticks along the fences in my mind (funny how darkness looks in upon itself and names it 'other'). The quiet of some days is just too much.

Your legs above the earth are as strange as your heart sunk below. Do the hills rise into the sky for you? If you can find the secrets in your wounds to open up to me, I will tell them everything you need them to know. This splintered curtain of spectacular glass across your face still cuts me. Why is it I cannot stop peeling my own when I think of you? I had almost forgotten the way the sunlight fades through in diamond-shaped slivers. When you speak I still listen for you, I'm sure it's then you deepen the rasp in your voice.

I would have done anything for the way you wore that sound.

Your ebony rose gardens have overgrown my ivory body. I suck on the rustblood of their succulent thorns, their petals crush as softly as summer midnight lakes filling the holes in my sadness. Everything about you was soil they neglected. Everything you left was torment I can't believe they buried.

I do not sleep but have been forced to wander dreams. We meet; we separate.

They could not understand you, that is what I understood about you most. You, the angel in my murderous hour, remind me what love with iron claws is like on fire flaring up inside my wrists. Speak for me the terrors they tear open the ground to exhume. It has been so long since this kind of glow remembered a creature as faint as me. When I think of the dance I think of us. When I think of the end I pray it traces away the waif I have become.

While they count syllables you have moved on, you begin to dictate the waves along the shore. While they grow tired and I grow distant I sense you at my heels, you at my tableside, you shadow of my shadow, you purgatory's music of peculiar beat.

— for the one come back to life.

Let the darkness
within me
be the ink
for if it is only darkness
I cannot breathe.

I am afraid
I do not know how
to count backwards from
I might be
losing you.

If it is not falling for you
as you look it dead in the eye
it is
not poetry.

Where were you
when I needed
the sound
of your madness.

You are so good to me, I press the words like secrets against your neck. You part my lips with your fingers and as my chin drips into your madness I catch a glimpse of the knives behind the eyes. A thin shimmer of blades, a sparkle in the way this will end badly for both of us but what are the endings if not the beginnings.

We have been here before, rough hands grazing my silk stomach. I know every move you make before you make it, I can practically sing to it. You, whistling for me in the darkness which cradles itself.

For all the sweetness hanging from the cliffs between us, threaded in honey currents beneath my fevered skin, poets only attempt to touch the things we know we cannot reach. Such arrogance, such hope. For all we expose even more is forbidden. We the fire in the ice in the raindrops trailing along your spine.

Time is a twisted punishment but you are so beautiful when you close your eyes.

This is love, this is lust, but this is not the answer. No such thing. Just the breathing out and breathing in, we are steel traps with ripening skin.

This is the life and death of the mind inside the mind, the body inside the body in constant rotation. There is nothing to see but the way we see it. Tomorrow is already here, beloved, (eating us eating us eating us) it's the horizon which never comes.

Day breaks where loneliness mouths the word for freedom. Quiet fog in your glass house. Cherry wine in your torn up throat, blood washing itself in the curtains.

We will always be lost within a journey into our own abyss.

We will always go hungry feasting upon ourselves.

— stranger dark.

We did not know
that the only things that
would ever matter
were the things we lost
inside ourselves
thinking,
so mistakenly,
that we had to choose
between breathing
or facing
the pain.

— breathe.

Your lips searching me
opening secrets
I am too afraid
to speak.

There is nothing outside of us
that is not within us.

This is our greatest
barrier to love

and our greatest
invitation
to it.

You cannot lose, beloved,
if you enter into it
already grateful.

All those creative, expressive, soulful things we hold back, we swallow and force down, because we are afraid of judgment. Their courageous way forward is your gratitude for them in yourself, your gratitude for being here and able to share them. What you offer in gratitude is already won, already a success, already worthy, already true, already beautiful.

The writer's most important gift
is that she believes.

She believes in the next word.
She believes in what she has summoned
and what she has laid to rest.

She believes in what she cannot yet see but knows in her bones
is on its way to her.

Notebooks on bedside tables are faith.

Quiet hours alone are prayers.

And behind every passage before it is written
moves the hand of her god.

I have been broken
a thousand times
just today.

Just to get here and stand in front of you and offer you the joy I
carry in my hands in spite of the fear which lines the cracks in my
skin, and invite you to move in step, in space, with me, I have cut
off the heads of jealousy, insecurity, doubt, ache, uncertainty, and
tucked away a deep immovable sadness.

Some of the pain, the little shards I just could not seem to let go
of, some is still here with me, pin pricks against my fingertips, little
burns behind my listless eyes, tiny blisters on my empty tongue,
a string of blue bruises dangling up and down my throat, each
whisper about me and whirl against the charcoal backdrop
of my lonely mind.

And you are here and not here.
And you ask and do not ask.
And we both smile softly to help
find our feet as we do
and do not
move on.

All I ever wanted
was to tell you a story
that feels like a lover
you've not yet
breathed against.

Blessed are we
the wounded.
The ones who sense
the coming storm
and do not run.

It will take time.
And a deeper amount
of gentleness
than you have yet
imagined possible.

— becoming home to yourself.

When I spoke of the light
they told me I was
dreaming.

When I spoke of the dark
they told me I was
tragic.

When I spoke to you
you welcomed all of it
and told me I

was everything.

Morning rain is gentle and steady upon my face as I huddle into myself, thankful finally for a day without sun. For the most part, I find daylight too harsh. It interrupts my sense of what is beautiful. Who could I ever tell that shadows help me find the most dazzling silhouettes of light.

My mind is wandering (which, really, sounds too calm because my mind, she whirrs and trips over herself and cascades to places I would rather not say). I do not speak the way I am supposed to, I speak too much like fire and ice and volcanoes. I do not understand the language of the stars which birthed me. I do not speak words bred of tenderness anymore without turning this tongue into blades.

Rewards become punishments.

To sink is to swim.

It's now and it's never and it's always in-between.

If I lose track of who is winning will you still let me in? I get so tired of keeping score. I get so sick of counting doors along hallways which never seem to end. All these floors hidden underneath the scaffolding around your heart, all these thick windows which slip away from me fall and crash and descend as I am cut, I am bruised, I am a shattered face on the inside of the muse.

But if I look deep enough, there is you. And you just keep rising up and up above dark clouds and I wonder why we try any more to place these blistered feet upon the ground. Will you run, will you stay, will you break as I have. Who will save us now when the walls are oceans splitting in half.

As I write this, all the lives I have since let go of drift off and I remember a time when I mistook the perfume of your secrets for nourishment. You who collects hearts in mouths and swallows their tears one by one, slow.

You the one who digs the claws of adoration in like furious flashes of heat across the summer lightning in my veins, you could have me and it breaks my heart you don't want me anymore. When exactly does that shift? What rock face crumbles away from my self disclosure against which you suddenly decide if this is madness it suits me, not you.

And somehow the chaos appears to reduce you only slightly.

And somehow I have become the one fading from view.

— this chaos it suits you.

You seem to be waiting
for permission.
My beloved,
I tell you this:
there is no such thing.

So write all of it.
Even as many people
come and go
as they adore and forget you
as they question you and open you
and move on.
As they stay.
Do not worry about them.
You are still this heavy beautiful
collection of dark skies
stealing catches of light
through trees.

All of my words
were feathers.
Intimate secrets
placed upon the wind.

I don't mind
the way we break.
I like the way my pieces
catch the light.

No, beloved,
bloom right here.
In the muck and the mess
and the rubble.
That the ones who brave
the darkness
may find you.

— bloom.

We were delicate
we were intricate
we were each other's
only way home.

Love me
until it hurts.
Open me as wide
as the world is broken.

All we ever truly seek
is love.
Whatever the ache
it seeks love.

Whatever the ache
it seeks love.
Whatever appears as self-destruction
is a cry for a return to love.
There is no other craving.
Every pain
every tear
every thirst
every hunger
is a quest for deeper love.

Do not judge your pain
or the way it is trying to capture
your attention.
The soul cannot help
but try to heal itself
through you.

Turn toward what hurts, be not afraid
to touch yourself there.
This is healing.
This is self-compassion.
This is your jagged
beautiful journey
home.

Please stop
leaving your skies
inside me
like scars.

My faith
is simply this:
that love
has never left me.

It's hard sometimes
to sit alone in a room and love yourself all the way down.
Down where the fears pool inside the caves you would rather turn
away from.
Down where the body submits to the dark madness of the universe
which spins you at will, takes your curiosity and opens it wider than
time and space.

As we approach the guiding lights of love, the painful bits within
heat up and are burned away as we get closer to our own healing.

It's not easy to sink into yourself and believe that you are worthy of
the breath that animates your entire life, the temporary heart which
beats like wings against the fragile air. There is a jaggedness to this
kind of deliberate stillness, this disciplined silence, the feeling that
at any moment you will fall backwards into the truth and the full
power of who you are.

That sensation of letting go of something you don't hold with
your hands but with the desperate clutches of your own illusions,
can feel frightening.

I guess I have always had a little flame of faith, a strange unyielding
core belief in something I know created me in its kindness, in its
likeness, in the taste of its own consummate desire to be birthed as
a creature of flesh and bone and skin, and I only feel sustained by
brushing up against it as often as I can.

To sit with my own humility, to drink from the pulsing current of
my own Divine grace.

Even as I fall something falls with me and it is not afraid of
anything.

It has a million intricate manifestations
but as the quiet nestles against me

I know my faith is simply this:
that love has never left me.

— meditation.

Let this be, child.
Let this be what it is.
This light and this darkness
as they are
becoming.
Fold your pulse
into the hands
of the mystery
and be open
be listening.

You unlock your mouth in dreams
undone by my adoration,
my heart continues
to divide.

What may I offer you to feast upon?
This body is sacred, this body is sick.

I drip as you beg
at the plastic edges of my sweet disturbance,

cry for the softmilk of my blood.

The pallid grasp of chemical hands
drowning the streets in her venomous drink,
sing for the weakness of thy flesh,
how charming the scent of dark, ripe seed.

In the place where love has never lived,
the mourning of love grows here:
spread wide and sodden atop the fading gravestone hills,
a cold nightwind gives birth

to a dying winter sky

our pleasured anguish writhing
beautifully beneath her.

— beg.

luminae

In tender dreams
we are love
without hands
without faces.
Our mouths
dark heaven
our bodies
tempestuous sky.

I will take you
without the smile.
I will take you
whatever is under the mask
 you wear.
I will take you
into these arms
and the beating of this heart will take you
so far
away from here
to a place where we
can take everything off
and lay everything down
and they can't ever reach
or hurt
us now.

What is true
is often the quietest sound
in all the world.
What is true is that which
whispers inside you
now.

You must hold yourself
in all weather
as if
you were the
softest
thing
in all the universe.

I run
from the things
which sustain me.
I take up my body and soul
and abandon the things
that want to cradle me.
Have you any idea
how brutal that
sounds?

I think they are probably going to leave. It will be a thing you said as your eyes slid clear past them to the corner of the room, or it will be a thing you didn't say when they looked to you for the answer you did not yet know how to give.

It isn't their fault, of course, it's just how they were built. How most of us were built. The cravings for fast, easy, beautiful things to numb the pain. The way they never turn their heads these days, you know that wasn't how they came. I once met a man who could turn his head clear all the way around like an owl; he could do it without getting twisted up at all it was nonsense and so frightening it was inspiring.

We were born one way but now we have become the raging discomfort of what they have impaled upon us. The way you speak, the way you think, the questions you do not have the guts to ask, how much of it is your own? What would you tell them if there were only five bodies in the streets? If there were five hundred thousand men, women and children of every race, color and creed. Would that change the depth of your message or just the size of the audience?

What builds us up tears us apart. What is walking toward us is walking toward walking away.

Here they come with their guns and their poetry. Here they come with their sunburns and cures for the common ignorance.

And here is you with your hands all on my early grave. Here is you with your tongue all down my throat. Here we stand face to face without one fucking single thing to say.

I'm not sure when I fell apart but I must have. Because everyone I meet is handing me shreds of things I do not ask for but they seem to think I need.

Every way I turn I'm kicking up pieces of whatever this is which has shattered itself to morph into me.

— becoming of age.

So this
is delicacy.
So this
is where
lace
becomes bone.

This beauty within me
how she aches
wondering why
I am so afraid.

I am without
the words.
The world does not
exist
when I am
this way.

Do not accept
the silence
where there should
be screams
nor the screams
where there should
be singing
nor the singing
where it does not
belong.

— stand.

The way we return
is the way
we began.
As miracles
as tiny breaks in the ground
as wilderness.

What will you do
with the coming true
of us.

Where is it
we think
we come from
if not
from love.

She escapes
sometimes
when the world
gets too loud
within
her.

Where you are afraid
where it hurts
to look
where your light
seems tangled
in the dark
I will meet you there
and we will hold the night
inside the breath between us
and curl our souls around
the way
the stars
look to us
for healing.

The future has always
been dark, beloved.
Always unknown
and unknowable.
Dark
that we may be
the burning lights
and be seen.

And so it came to settle into the flesh. Autumn warmth had been taught to neglect the nectarine sky, dark ivy gardens like iron mistakes, the softest for beheadings.

This had been coming for some time but they never tell you how it will feel. Train tracks storming the cross center of the chest. Fevered moth wings stirring up
the swell in your throat.

And the way you touch me, there and there and here,
rain moves into sunlight, wet stains upon your face
peels her teeth against the curtains, like pale eyelids eloping.

With you everything drips of descending, velvet stair cases for miles sinking to the bottom of the sea. The heels of gravity throwing lakes into stones, the dull pink tongues of gulls and we, always hungry.
If you part your lips enough that would be all you ever need to say.

Me
forever spinning collarbones looking for a way
back into the shell of who I used to be.

You
the extension of all the words unspoken between us
thunder between the mountains and the sun.

Cry for daybreak.

Cry for love,
she is in the parlor room bleeding.

Eyes always too protruding. Hands around the air we breath.

Nothing to keep us together.
Nothing for an ending to embrace.

— cry for love.

My skin stays awake
for a taste of you.

— in dreams.

If you do not
judge your darkness
she will not
betray you.

I am in love with the promise of another morning.

If it is cruel it is not brave.

Poetry
is a lifestyle.
It is not something
that ever leaves.

Along the dusted edges
of a world unknown
bodies trailing by
I walk as though a secret

as though a memory
an ivory mist between the fingers
a dream of a time to come
not promised, not spoken of.

We hold onto hope the way we bow our bright eyes into the fog, made in the image of ghosts, made of wisps of fading photograph delirium, the glow at the tips of fireflies against water in the dark. Reflections. Illusions. For everything we hold we wish were something else.

If we are not lovers, if we are not bound together by vein or tongue or country, if our visions eclipse each other but do not touch, then let the world be brought into eternal solitude, let the earth beneath my grass wet feet weep only to be alone. There is something here we refuse to see. Something intelligent, calling to us with its mouth, a wide gray ocean, fingers tearing open knees, rain pricks stiff along the neck beneath the trees.

And we drift, we are adrift, we grasp for what we cannot believe only to fall again upon ourselves. This is me against me. This is you against you, and every mirror is another hall. The rolling thunder of this bone longing, this desperation. Press your palms to mine, I can feel your heart bleeding into time. And as the sun turns down her body to blue sing the mountains to sleep, I am a wanderer inside for the way we do not see.

A vessel for the silence crawling along the seams.

— this is what I love, this right here.

It is your work
which will make you rejoice
for this life of yours
the one breathing
in your hands.
Make no mistake
if it does not bring you
a deep and gutting joy
if it does not glisten
the wild
back into your blood
if it does not feed you
magic
from the tips of its fingers
or whisper you awake
to drink of the moon
in the deadness of night
it is not
your work.

— what you came here to do.

I felt an overpowering need to be alone with something impossible to name. It had hands clutched full of the flesh of silence which multiplied without end. There was no one in that place. Everyone had left and they had each pulled one of its doors shut behind them. I was very alone. It was very dark, it was very peaceful, I was afraid. I was very afraid it would end and that it would never end. It was womanlike and dim, a love that could only breathe you out and breathe you in this way. It could only flower in solitude. It would only expose itself one to one, face to face, mouth to mouth.

A mysterious union which was without need for bodies, it was body-less. Forbidden and yet met with an almost primitive expectation. The pain and terror of all the world rested its head in this place.

An apex. A resuscitation.

It was a life invading itself where death had long been its only comfort.

I have carried the buds of a thousand gardens inside of me, many lifetimes have I been caressed against my will. I have produced and offered the milk and the honey, the fire and the water and the abuse. I have been unable to bloom, longing to encircle my thick vines around the precious feet of the marbled gray daylight.

All I want now is to be alone with this unknowable thing and to let it feel me, I want to feel inside of it with my tongue, with my fingers, with my body and blood, with my consciousness and my subconsciousness, in waking and in dreams, to penetrate it with the poison which consumes me and give it a punishing pleasure. I want to stretch into its glistening web and learn to obey the strange fluid rhythms of its body-less pulse.

We speak too loudly and too often. We are murdering something which cannot leave. I cannot bear any longer to sleep outside of it. There is a place beyond this one, it lives inside. It hopes no one will come to the door. It hopes no one will understand its words, it wants to close in around itself and return the light to its tomb underground. It gives birth to its own time. It chews its own limbs and destroys its own space. It wants to make love to the darkness and water its wings with the tears that fall like petals from the last sighs of the last stars. It is perpetual. It does not name what it wants.

— it does not name what it wants.

We are delivered
womb into womb.

Be gentle.

We are not yet
fully formed.

I'd rather be silent.

Don't you worry
about them,
angel.
Just keep dancing
like you do.

Let them talk.
Let them stare.
Let them judge.
Let them be.

Because when the world
feels like it is closing
in
it will be
the dancing
that sets
you free.

I write in the mornings
of days other people
throw away.
Maybe
I write for them.

I guess I have always
had a thing
for the underdog.
The ones who say the most
breathtaking things
when hardly anyone is listening.
The ones who do the most good
when no one
is cheering them on.
We have all been there.
Forget everything you have heard
about what beautiful is.
Beautiful is a struggle.
A brash determination
to begin
from the mess
of where you are
when no one
is looking.

You are a beautiful
beginning
even when
no one
is
looking.

I like the gray
days
faces
shadows
skies.
They break you
and hold you
just enough.

How impossible
how disruptive
how beautiful
this conversation
we might have
been.

I think art is
a conversation
we have with our soul.
The kind we cannot
have
with anyone else.

I want you
to go make your art.
I do not want you
to miss out
on
yourself.

When you are cradling
the words
and realize
they are saving you.

There will always be a part of you
that will never be seen
or understood
by anyone else.
Take deep
prolific comfort
in that part.
Create and share
as honestly and boldly as you can
but never forget that part.
Never wish that part away.
No matter what happens
respect
honor
cherish
and
protect
that part.

That part's yours.

When everything else
finally closes
the seed
of the soul
falls open.

Made in the USA
Monee, IL
01 September 2022

13028192R00152